THE POWDER MONKEY

MAUREEN RYLANCE

Illustrated by Robin Lawrie

For Jessica

PACIFIC LEARNING

© 2001 Pacific Learning
© 1999 Written by **Maureen Rylance**
Illustrated by **Robin Lawrie**
US Edit by **Alison Auch**

This Americanized Edition of *The Powder Monkey* ,
originally published in English in 1999, is published
by arrangement with Oxford University Press.

05 04 03 02 01
10 9 8 7 6 5 4 3 2 1

Published by
Pacific Learning
P.O. Box 2723
Huntington Beach, CA 92647-0723
www.pacificlearning.com

ISBN: 1-59055-078-1

PL-7604

This book uses some words that may be
unfamiliar. These words are set in italics, and you can
find their meanings in the Glossary on page 95.

Contents

1

Getting Ready to Sail

Harry looked at the rat. It was on the shelf in front of him. Its beady eyes stared and its long whiskers twitched. He banged on the shelf with his fist, and the rat vanished behind some sacks.

Harry loved the storeroom of the ship's *chandler*. It was dusty and gloomy and the air was heavy with all kinds of smells, but to Harry it was a really interesting place. He could put up with a few rats and cockroaches. He planned to go to sea in a couple of years, and he knew he would see plenty of those.

He looked around the storeroom. It was crammed to the hilt with bundles, sacks, barrels, and containers. Whatever captains wanted for their ships, they could get it here. Everyone said that Shadrach Pinchbeck had the finest chandler's store in the county. When Harry was captain of his own ship, he would buy his supplies here.

In two more years he would be thirteen. Then no one could keep him from joining the King's Navy. He could hardly wait.

Harry suddenly realized that Shadrach was calling him.

"Come on, lad, what are you doing? There's work to be done."

Harry sighed and dragged a roll of sail canvas down from a shelf. He staggered into the shop and set it down on the floor. When Shadrach wasn't looking, he took a quick peek out at the harbor.

People bustled around. The stallkeepers were doing a fine trade, and there was a buzz of excitement in the air.

His Majesty's ship, the *Prosperity*, was getting ready to set sail. Its crew were going into battle to fight the French – to defend the country.

"Now, lad, I won't put up with daydreamers," Shadrach said. "Do you want to earn two pennies today or not?"

"Oh yes, sir! I'm sorry," said Harry. He knew how pleased his ma would be when he brought home two precious pennies.

"All right. I'll read out the rest of the things from the list, and you go into the back and bring them out."

Shadrach moved around carefully, dodging the hundreds of jugs, pots, and canisters that hung from every part of the ceiling.

"Move fast, mind you, or I'll let some other little scallywag have your job."

"This is a lot of stuff for one ship," Harry said, looking at the pile of supplies on the floor.

"Well, a fine ship such as the *Prosperity* needs plenty of supplies to keep officers and crew going. Who knows how long they'll be away? And this is only part of it. They'll get the rest from the navy yard." Shadrach licked his pencil, and made marks on his list.

"All right, what's next? Ah, of course, eight lanterns and at least two boxes of sailmaker's needles."

Harry ran into the musty storeroom again. When he returned, Shadrach was talking to a large, rough-looking man. His navy jacket had several brass buttons missing, and he had a dirty black scarf knotted around his neck. In his hand, he held a short length of twisted rope. Suddenly, he brought the rope down hard on to some sacks. Clouds of dust rose in the air. Harry jumped and stumbled back into the doorway of the storeroom.

"Aye, that's a fine enough cat-o'-nine-tails," the man said with a satisfied air. "I usually make my own, but time's pressing. I'll have three more. I'll likely need them on this trip. There are always cowards who'll run away from hard work or a battle."

He grinned, showing a mouth full of brown and black teeth. "The captain wants to know how much longer you'll be," the man said. "He wants to set sail on tonight's tide."

"Everything will be ready in two hours," Shadrach replied.

After he had gone, Shadrach stood with his hands on his hips. He shook his head. "There goes a cruel man, Harry," he said.

"Who is he, sir?" Harry asked.

"That's the ship's *bosun*, from the *Prosperity*. I feel for the poor men working under him."

"What was that rope thing he wanted?"

"The cat-o'-nine-tails has been used to strike fear into the heart of many a man." Shadrach shook his head again.

Harry stared at him. "In the King's Navy?"

"Yes, it's a cruel world, lad," he said, "and folks don't always get what they deserve." He looked at the list. "Get me two sets of signaling flags and a box of candles."

2

Monkey Business

The next hour flew by. Harry's arms and legs ached. He never stopped running and carrying, and he was glad when Shadrach sent him on an errand to the gunsmith.

He loved going to Jeremiah Mumford's shop. He would get to see George. George was his best friend, even though he was twenty years old. He had been teaching Harry to read and write and work with numbers.

"Ask Mr. Mumford if I can have some *wads* for the large cannons," Shadrach said. "And don't stand gawking at that ship while you're out. Be quick."

Harry ran along the *quay*, dodging between the people who were still coming and going. On his left, he passed the swordsmith, the tailor, and the printer. There on his right was the dock, and in the dock was His Majesty's ship, *Prosperity*.

It towered over everything and everybody. Harry had to tilt his head back as far as he could to see the top of the great masts. Each time he looked, it took his breath away. He could see the mighty cannons poking from the gunports along the side of the ship.

He closed his eyes and imagined that he was part of the brave crew, going off to fight for their country with the famous Lord Nelson, Fleet Admiral.

He watched the sailors climbing the rigging. He admired the groups of officers, standing around and talking, or parading back and forth in their neat uniforms.

Harry would go on a ship like that. Why should he worry about the cat-o'-nine-tails? He would be the best sailor they ever had.

He hurried to the gunsmith. As always, he looked up at the fine painted sign above the door: Jeremiah Mumford, Supplier of Ball and Shot to His Majesty's Navy.

"Well, hello there, young Harry," said Mr. Mumford in a jolly voice. "Shadrach will be busy today, I'll bet."

Harry smiled and greeted Mr. Mumford. "Mr. Pinchbeck asked if he could please have some wads for the large cannons."

"Aye, I expect they're for the *Prosperity*, are they? They say it sets sail tonight."

"Yes, sir," Harry said.

Mr. Mumford went into the back room. Soon afterward, George came out.

"Hello, Harry. Do you have time for some writing practice? I left the top line of today's accounts blank so that you can write in the date if you like."

They went into the office. Harry looked around. George laughed.

"Don't worry," he said, "she's still here." He pointed to the tall bookshelves.

There, perched on the top shelf, was a small brown monkey. She was watching Harry. Her bright little eyes blinked as George lifted a lantern so that Harry could see better. The monkey started to chatter softly.

"May I feed her?" Harry asked.

"When you've done your writing practice," George said. "I've got some fruit you can give her."

George placed a huge book on the desk and pointed to the top of a page. Harry often wrote in the ledger, and he was getting very good. George had said that soon no one would be able to tell the difference between Harry's writing and his own.

Harry picked up the pen and dipped it into the ink. He licked his lips as he worked. Carefully, he shaped each letter: *October 4, 1805*.

When he finished, George nodded his head. It was a fine piece of writing. "Well, I suppose I'd better get that fruit," he said.

Harry looked around for the monkey. She had come down to a lower shelf.

Mr. Mumford came in. "That monkey's a little nuisance," he said. "I don't know what to do with her now that my good lady's tired of her. I might have to give away the little thing." Harry's eyes widened.

Mr. Mumford looked at Harry's writing in the ledger. "Well done, lad. There'll be a job here for you one day, if you want it. That is, if your head's not still full of going to sea."

George returned with an apple. He used his pocket knife to cut it into small slices. The monkey chattered excitedly

"I've seen too many people go off in a ship and never come back," Mr. Mumford said.

"Oh, Mr. Mumford," Harry said politely, "I'd rather fire guns than make them."

George shook his head.

Mr. Mumford laughed. "I remember feeling the same way myself, Harry, when I was your age – until I understood how terrible war can be. You'll grow out of it."

Harry silently promised himself he would not.

As George and Mr. Mumford talked about the price of gunpowder, Harry took the pieces of apple from George and walked over to the shelves.

The little monkey hopped up and down. She reached out and tried to snatch some slices from Harry's hands. Harry closed his hand tightly. The monkey screamed at him. Slowly, Harry opened his fingers. This time, the monkey very gently took a piece and popped it into her mouth. "Have you thought of a name for her, sir?" Harry asked.

"No. She seems quite happy to be just Monkey," the gunsmith said.

"Would you let me give her a name, sir?" Harry asked.

"Can't see why not. Tell you what, next time I see you, tell me what her name is to be."

Harry smiled and thanked him.

Mr. Mumford pointed to a framed sampler on the wall. "See that, lad? Mrs. Mumford sewed that for me. Can you read it?"

"There's no place like home," Harry read.

"Exactly. You remember those words," the gunsmith said. "The navy's not for anyone who wants to live long and be happy."

"Sir, what shall I tell Mr. Shadrach about the wads?" Harry said, eager to change the subject.

"Tell him I'll send them over to him in half an hour."

Harry thanked Mr. Mumford and waved to George. He took one last look at the monkey, and said good-bye.

George called after him. "I'll not be giving you a lesson tonight, Harry. I'm going out to meet with some mates."

"Now don't do that, young George," said Mr. Mumford. "Only fools will be out and about tonight. Home is the best place to be on the night that one of His Majesty's ships sets sail."

"Why is that, Mr. Mumford?" Harry asked.

"Never you mind, boy, and I hope you never find out. Now get back to your master."

3

A Warning

Shadrach was looking at the huge piles of stores waiting to be taken to the *Prosperity*.

"Well, that's a job well done, Harry. We've earned our money today. I'll get you your two pennies and then you can go."

Harry sat on a barrel to wait.

A loud voice from behind startled him so much that he tumbled onto the dusty floor. "Well, boy, don't just sit there. Get your master. Tell him Mr. Swan is here to see him."

It was the bosun.

"Yes, sir," Harry said, and he ran off to get Shadrach.

As the two men talked, Harry watched and listened from the storeroom door.

Mr. Swan, the bosun, called outside to some men. They came in and began to heave the barrels and boxes onto their strong shoulders.

Mr. Swan strode over to Harry and took him by the arm.

"You too, lad. Give us a hand. It might give you some real muscles. You're like a bundle of bones."

He gripped Harry's arm so firmly that Harry felt like telling him to let go, but he kept his mouth shut.

"Er, Bosun, the lad's still needed here. He hasn't finished his work," Shadrach lied.

"Now then, Chandler, am I to tell my captain you're not being helpful?" He smiled, showing his rotting teeth. "If I say the lad helps, then that's the way it is," he said angrily. He pushed past Shadrach.

"All right, Mr. Swan," Shadrach said, "but I can't spare him for long." He looked at Harry. "Better do as he says, son."

"Bring those boxes," the bosun snapped. He walked out of the shop.

Shadrach pulled Harry to one side and whispered to him. "Now listen, Harry, just go as far as the gangplank. No matter what happens, do not go on the ship. Do you hear me? Don't go on the ship."

Harry understood the look on his face. "All right, sir," he said. "I won't."

Shadrach lifted the boxes and put them into Harry's outstretched arms.

4

On Board

The boxes were heavy, but Harry was determined to keep up with the line of sailors. Everyone on the quay made way for them as they walked by.

"Don't let the French get away with anything!" the pie stallkeeper called as they passed.

"Don't you worry," one of the sailors called back. "Our big cannons will ride roughshod over Nappy's Navy. This war with the French has been going on too long."

Harry knew that Nappy's Navy meant Napoleon's Navy.

Napoleon was the leader of the French, and he was trying to conquer all of Europe. Lord Nelson was the leader of the English forces, and he was trying to defend the country against a French invasion. George had told him that.

When the loading party reached the gangplank, they had to wait. Some sailors were leading sheep aboard. Others were carrying crates of squawking chickens.

"Are they going to be cooked for your meals?" Harry asked the seaman next to him.

The man laughed out loud. "No, son," he said. "That meat would be too good for the likes of us. It's salt beef and maggot-ridden biscuits for us."

"Maggots?" Harry said.

A sailor pushed him roughly in the back. "Out of the way, monkey," he said.

"Don't call me a monkey," Harry called back.

The first seaman laughed. "He thinks you're a *powder monkey*," he said to Harry.

"What's a powder monkey?" Harry said.

"It's a…"

The rest of his words were lost in the shouts of the sailors as they moved onto the gangplank.

Harry stopped. He desperately wanted to go on the ship, but he knew he should do as Shadrach had told him. He put down the boxes and turned to go.

Suddenly, he was grabbed by the collar of his shirt. He felt it rip across his shoulder.

"Where do you think you're going, you idle little brat?" It was the bosun.

"I've got to go back to the chandler's," Harry answered nervously.

"Pick up those boxes and take them on board, before I make you."

Harry decided to do as he was told. He struggled up the gangplank, trying not to trip.

It was hard to see where he was going, with the boxes he was carrying. Sailors pushed rudely past him.

Finally, he stepped off the gangplank and on to the deck of the ship.

He felt thrilled. He was actually on board the great fighting ship, *Prosperity*. If the bosun hadn't been so close by, Harry could have enjoyed the moment and taken a good, long look around.

"See that?" the bosun growled at him, pointing to a ladder that led down from the deck.

"Take the boxes down, then get back up here for some more."

Harry had seen the other sailors go down this ladder. They had balanced the boxes and bundles on their shoulders. It looked easy enough, but the ladder seemed very narrow.

Carefully, he heaved two boxes to his shoulder and turned to go down the ladder. It was very difficult because he could only hold on with one arm.

As he started to climb below the level of the lower deck, he listened to the bosun's footsteps as he walked off.

Shaking with the effort and excitement, he reached the bottom. He looked around the gloomy areas of belowdecks. There was a horrible stale smell that made him catch his breath.

"This must be the hold," he muttered to himself. It was a little like the storeroom at the chandler's, piled high with boxes and barrels and crates.

He set his boxes on a barrel, but before he could climb back out, he heard a voice.

"Look out below!"

He jumped out of the way as some sacks were lowered by rope.

"You two get down there and stack those sacks properly. Get those barrels lashed together as well," yelled the bosun. "I'll be down in a minute."

"Aye, aye, sir," came the reply, and two sailors came down into the hold.

Harry didn't want to catch the bosun's eye again, so he decided to hide behind the barrels. The stacks of boxes wobbled as he crouched down.

He was just in time. The two sailors untied the sacks and stacked them in front of the barrels. He heard the bosun come heavily down the ladder.

"Now then, you two, I've got a special job for you tonight. You'll need a couple of mates to help you."

The sailors made no reply.

"There'll be extra rations for you and money in your pocket if you do the job right," he went on.

"Is it the usual job?" one asked, spitting on the floor.

"Aye," the bosun said, "the captain needs at least twenty more crew, and our little group has to get half of them. So I want you to come with me to the taverns, and we'll talk some likely lads into joining." He gave a cruel laugh. "Know what I mean, lads? If they're not too keen, just show them this, and don't, under any circumstances, take 'no' for an answer." He laughed again.

Harry peeped out to see what the bosun was holding up. It was a wooden club.

The bosun pushed it toward the chin of one of the sailors. The sailor staggered back into the sacks, then he fell backward against Harry's barrel.

"Meet me on the quay in half an hour," the bosun growled, and he climbed up to the main deck.

The sailor righted himself, but the barrel tipped back, and the boxes that Harry had hurriedly put on top of them slid off. One of them crashed down on his head. He felt a sharp pain, and his stomach heaved. Then the room around him faded into blackness.

5

An Unexpected Journey

Harry woke in a panic. His mouth was dry, and he thought he was suffocating. It was dark except for a very faint light coming from somewhere above him.

Something soft brushed against his face. Then something ran across his chest. He cried out. He brushed at his shirt and sharp teeth bit at his hand. He screamed.

As he tried to get up, the floor dipped sharply to his left and he rolled over. He crashed into something heavy.

Trying to catch his breath, he lay as still as he could. Slowly, the floor dipped the other way, and Harry tried to keep himself from rolling again.

Through the gloom, he saw boxes, sacks, barrels, and huge coils of rope. Then he spotted the dozen or more creatures swarming around him. Rats!

He kicked out wildly and waved his arms. They scurried away behind the barrels. Fear made him breathless. He tried to calm himself, but he wished the floor would stop moving. Something was terribly wrong.

It was only when he became aware of the regular creaking sounds of the wooden ship, that he realized the awful truth.

Not only was he still aboard the *Prosperity*; it had set sail. He was at sea!

He touched his sore head and he tried hard to remember what had happened. Soon, everything began to come back to him. He thought of his ma and Shadrach wondering where he was. The thought almost brought tears to his eyes. What was he going to do?

He looked up toward the light. He knew he would have to climb up there and find someone to help him. He hoped it wouldn't be the bosun.

Climbing the ladder was difficult because of the roll of the ship. At the top, he peered around the deck. The air didn't seem any better than down in the hold. The place was gloomy, lit by only two or three lanterns.

Here and there he saw men sitting and talking. Some were cleaning long lengths of heavy cable, others were playing a game.

They threw dice from a cup made of coiled rope, and they shouted at each other. Not far from the ladder, Harry saw some men in hammocks that were slung between the beams.

Taking a deep breath, he clambered from the ladder on to the deck. The ship heaved to one side and he stumbled, falling against one of the hammocks.

"Now then, lad," a voice called out, "take it easy."

"Sorry," Harry mumbled.

The sailor looked at Harry's worried face and laughed. "The first trip's always the worst, son. You'll soon get used to it."

"I'm not supposed to be here," Harry said, trying to keep his calm.

The sailor just laughed. "Get in your hammock and rest while you can. You have a chance to be on rat-catching duty in a couple of hours."

"I don't have a hammock," Harry said, staggering around as the ship dipped again.

"Well you can't sleep on the deck. You'll spend the night rolling around like a ball. You could lash yourself to one of the beams, if you like," the seaman said.

"Over here, son," another voice called out.

"You can have old Jem's hammock. He'll not be needing it anymore, poor old soul. May he rest in peace."

Harry muttered a thank you and scrambled toward the roll of canvas on the floor. A dead man's hammock was better than none.

The sailor showed Harry how to sling the canvas hammock between two beams.

Getting into it was the hardest part. The first three times he tried, he landed on the deck with a thud. On the fourth attempt, he managed to get in but immediately fell out the other side. He found himself laughing, in spite of everything.

"We'll make a sailor of you yet," the seaman said, smiling. "I'm Jack. Stick with me and you'll be all right," he added.

Harry thanked him and wriggled around in his new bed. The sides of the hammock seemed to fold around him, squeezing his arms to his side, but it was much better than rolling all over the deck. A few minutes later, he was fast asleep.

6

Fear and Excitement

Jack tipped Harry out of his hammock. Men were calling to each other and taking down their hammocks.

"Come on, lad, up on deck. You don't want the bosun to catch you down below after the shout." He pushed Harry up the ladder in front of him.

On the lower deck, there was a crowd of men. Harry stood behind Jack.

As he looked around him, he noticed other young boys. One of them looked really young. He had dark, curly hair and eyes that darted everywhere. When he saw Harry, he winked and gave him a wide grin. Harry found himself grinning back.

The bosun, Mr. Swan, was yelling orders. Men and boys raced off to carry out their tasks around the ship.

The bosun moved toward the last group. "Up to the top deck and get those animals slopped – now."

The boy with the grin leaped ahead of the men and climbed the ladder easily.

Harry tried desperately to keep himself hidden. He froze as he heard the bosun call out to Jack.

"You and the lad, get back down to the *orlop deck* and lend a hand to the surgeon." He laughed cruelly. "He's got quite a few injuries to attend to this morning."

"Aye, aye, sir," Jack said, and he dragged Harry back to the ladder.

The bosun hadn't recognized him, Harry realized. He felt overcome with relief. Perhaps things would be all right. This was what he wanted, wasn't it? He was on board one of His Majesty's ships. He was in the navy!

A tap from Jack's foot brought him back to reality. "Get a move on, lad."

On the gloomy, stale-smelling orlop deck, men were crouched on the floor. Some were holding their heads and groaning. Others just sat slumped forward, like half-empty sacks of grain. Harry noticed blood on them.

On one side of them hung a piece of dirty canvas acting as a curtain. From behind it came more groans.

"Who are they?" Harry asked Jack.

"Poor victims of the press-gangs, lad," he said. "That's how the captain gets some of his crew. Men like the bosun hit them over the head, then carry them on board. When they wake up, they're in the King's Navy."

Suddenly, Harry felt sick. A mixture of fear and excitement churned inside him.

The heavy atmosphere of the orlop deck was threatening to suffocate him. Foul smells filled his nostrils.

He wanted to be sick but his stomach was empty. He just made awful retching sounds that heaved at his stomach muscles. Jack touched his shoulder.

"Hey, lad, take it easy. We're here to help the doc, not to get treated ourselves."

Harry felt his strength ebb away. He sat down and Jack crouched beside him.

"What you need is something to eat. Didn't you have a good feed before you came aboard? Most young ones do."

Harry looked at Jack, and struggled to be brave. He didn't deserve to be on board a great ship like the *Prosperity*.

Jack pulled Harry to his feet and took him away from the waiting men.

"What's up, lad? You'd better tell me now – we've got work to do."

Harry bit his lip, and began telling Jack his story. When he'd finished, Jack ruffled his hair.

"No wonder you're feeling sorry for yourself. You should be back home with your ma."

"I really do want to be here," Harry protested. "It's just sort of sudden, you see. That's all."

Jack laughed. "Well then, welcome aboard, young sir. Now let's get on with our job, before the bosun catches us. Speaking of the bosun, you'd better keep out of his sight as long as you can."

For the next hour, Harry and Jack carried buckets of dirty water from behind the curtain up to the lower deck.

Once up there, they emptied the buckets overboard out of the gunports, where the great cannons stuck out of the sides of the ship.

The men were practicing loading and firing them. Whenever Harry passed the men, they glared at him.

Back on the orlop deck, he helped Jack fill the buckets with water from huge barrels.

He took them through the curtain, and as he did so, he stole a look at one of the seaman who was being treated by the doctor. His back was facing Harry.

The doctor appeared to be stitching up a wound on the young man's head. The man never made a sound.

"What are you gawking at?" the doctor growled at Harry.

Harry decided not to reply. He just scurried away through the curtain.

A few seconds later, the injured man came out. Harry looked at his pale face. He felt a shock go through him. The young man looked straight at him.

"Harry!" he exclaimed. "What on earth are you doing here?"

Harry smiled. "George!"

7

Rat Hunt

The young man and the boy hugged each other. Jack looked puzzled.

"Come over here where we won't be overheard. Tell me what's going on," he whispered.

Harry introduced George to Jack. While Jack watched for the bosun, Harry told George everything that had happened.

Then George told them his tale. He had gone out to meet with his friends. When he started on his way home, he had been jumped. He couldn't remember anything else. He had woken up aboard *Prosperity*.

"The press-gangs," said Jack. "Didn't anyone warn you about being out and about the night a ship sets sail?"

Harry and George looked at each other, remembering Mr. Mumford's warning.

"What do we do now?" George said, his face even paler than before.

"There's nothing you can do. Just grin and bear it. You're in the navy now, so you'd better make the best of it."

George gripped Harry's shoulder. "At least we're in it together. We'll help each other through."

"I reckon you need someone to keep an eye on both of you," Jack said.

He lifted one of George's hands. It was pale and smooth, with clean fingernails. He compared it to his own weathered, leathery hand with its dirty, ragged nails. "You've got the soft, uncalloused hands of a gentleman," he said.

"I work in a gunsmith's. I write up all the accounts," George explained.

Jack snorted. "What am I taking on? A gentleman and a…"

Harry thought he was about to say "baby," but Jack stopped and looked at him and smiled. "And a future captain of the King's Navy," he said, slapping Harry on the back, "with a bit of training from me, of course," he added.

The three of them laughed and shook hands with one another.

A loud voice called down to them: it was the bosun. He clattered down the ladder.

"Look lively there," he called. "Jack, you join gun crew number three. You new lads get down in the hold and get rid of some rats. I want twenty dead by the end of the watch, or there'll be trouble."

He went back up the ladder.

"Come on now, we've been chatting too long," Jack said.

Minutes later, Harry and George stood in the hold looking at each other. They held the thick pieces of wood Jack had given them.

"Have you ever killed a rat?" Harry asked. "I usually just scare them away."

"Yes, I have, but I can't say that I want to make a habit of it," George said, twisting his face. "How about you drive them out and I'll do the rest," he suggested.

Harry nodded.

About an hour later, Jack came down the ladder. They heard the sound of a bell ringing above them.

"It's the end of the watch. How many have you got?" Jack asked George.

George pointed to the dead rats on the floor. "Only nineteen," he said, shrugging his shoulders.

"Let's hope he doesn't count them," Jack said, looking worried.

He rummaged in his pockets and brought out a few biscuits. He offered them to Harry and George. They looked at the rats.

"Uh... I think we've lost our appetites," George said.

"You'll feel better when you're back on the orlop. Come on."

Jack helped George put the rats into a sack and they climbed the ladder.

The men were sitting at wooden tables or on the floor. Two of the sailors were giving out bowls and biscuits and pouring cider into tankards.

Jack found places for them at a table. He threw the sack of rats into a corner.

Harry noticed that the table was a broad plank, hanging from ropes attached to the wooden spars above. No matter how much the ship rolled around, the table hung there as level as could be. The bowls and tankards stayed in place.

"No cider for the lad," Jack said to the sailor pouring the drinks, and he covered Harry's tankard with his hand. "Plain water for you, Harry; the tasty stuff is reserved for the grown men."

Harry was disappointed. He wanted what the men had. Instead he got stale water.

Harry was surprised to find that he was hungry, and he crunched the hard cornmeal biscuit and looked for another. He munched happily as he listened to the men telling fascinating stories. He was just about to reach for another biscuit when he felt someone's eyes on him. The bosun was staring straight at him.

"Well, well, well," he said, "if it isn't the little bag of bones. How come you're still here?"

He reached out and pulled Harry to his feet. George began to rise from his seat, but Jack stopped him.

Harry swallowed his mouthful of biscuit, almost choking himself.

"And you, you pale-faced weakling," the bosun added, jabbing his hand into George's chest. "I've got something for you."

He picked up a sack from the floor and emptied it on to the table. The dead rats went everywhere. They sent the bowls of food and biscuits flying.

Harry's stomach churned as he looked at the sickening mixture of food and dead rats.

"Count them!" the bosun yelled at Harry.

His hands shook as he carefully counted the rats, pointing at each in turn.

The bosun's eyes narrowed as Harry reached the end of his count.

"Nineteen, sir," he said, his voice coming out in a whisper.

"I've a good mind to flog you both!" the bosun screamed at them. "I wanted twenty!"

"Just a minute, Bosun," said Jack. "I found a dead rat over in the corner near the sack. It must have fallen out. I'll get it for you."

Without another word, Jack went off and brought back another rat. George and Harry watched in amazement as he flung it on the table with the others.

The bosun glared at the three of them. "Get this mess cleared up," he said.

Then he pulled Harry to one side and pushed his face close up to him. "Now you're in the King's Navy, I've got just the job for you," he growled. "I will train you myself. We start in four hours."

"What am I to be, sir?" Harry asked.

The bosun laughed. "You, my lad, are going to be a powder monkey. What do you think of that?"

8
Powder Monkey

Jack told Harry all about powder monkeys. They were young boys who brought the cartridges of gunpowder to the cannons.

The cartridges were kept in a part of the hold called the magazine. The boys had to fill a leather carrying case with cartridges and climb with them up the ladders to the gun decks. The cartridges were then stored in a salt box until the gun crews loaded them into the cannons.

The boys had to be fast and be able to climb like monkeys.

Harry felt excited. It was such an important job, so he couldn't understand why George and Jack were looking so worried. He couldn't think of anything he'd rather be.

Even as the bosun dragged him to the middle deck, he didn't feel as frightened as he had before.

"Watch this gun crew practicing," the bosun ordered. They stood near a huge cannon, which the bosun told him was a twenty-four pounder.

"Watch everything they do and the order they do it. Learn it by heart, and keep a special eye on that monkey there. You'll replace him tomorrow."

Harry looked at the young boy. The boy had come quickly hurtling on to the deck and immediately emptied his bag of cartridges, stowing them safely in the salt box. Then off he went, disappearing below deck as quickly as if someone had tossed him down there.

For more than an hour, Harry watched the team of eight men. Each had his own job to do. They loaded, aimed, and pretended to fire the heavy black cannon.

The gun captain told him that when they really fired the gun, the recoil was so strong that it forced the cannon straight back several yards. Then the team would have to run the gun out again after each shot.

All this time, the young powder monkey flew up and down the ladders, bringing the cartridges. Now and again he would give Harry a tired smile.

When the bosun returned, Harry was fairly sure he understood the gun drill.

"The master says we can do it for real now," the bosun told the gun captain.

"Stand back," he told Harry, "and watch the experts at work. We can fire three shots to the French Navy's one."

The next few minutes were the most exciting of Harry's life. He watched as the sponge on the long stick was thrust into the barrel of the cannon. This was to put out any sparks still there from shots fired earlier.

Then a new cartridge was passed along and put into the cannon.

A member of the team, who was called the rammer, rammed it right into the barrel. Next a wad, just like the ones Mr. Mumford sold, was put in. Then a huge cannon ball was placed inside, and another wad after that.

Everything was ready for the fuse to be set and gunpowder poured into the top of the cannon.

Then some men aimed the cannon. They did this by wedging its barrel up or down, and heaving the gun carriage to the left or right with long *handspikes*.

All this was done in less than a minute.

The gun captain yelled, "Stand clear."

All of the gun crew leaped to the sides and cowered down. One of them grabbed Harry and pushed him down beside them. Seconds later, there was a shout.

"Fire!"

Then there was the biggest bang Harry had ever heard. The air around him seemed to quiver, and he coughed as he breathed in the thick, gritty smoke.

There was a loud rumbling sound as the huge cannon recoiled. It moved back almost fifteen feet!

Seconds later, the whole process began again. Harry's ears were ringing.

Before the next shot was fired, the bosun dragged Harry to the ladder. They went down to the orlop, then on down to the far end of the hold.

"This is the magazine," the bosun said. "You stay down here for a while and watch the monkey work."

He started to climb up the ladder but jumped out of the way as the powder monkey came scurrying down. Only when the boy was safely down did the bosun go up.

"He got out of the way for you," Harry gasped in amazement. "I thought he would trample on anyone who got in his way."

The young boy laughed.

"It's a ship's rule," he said breathlessly. "Get in the way of a powder monkey and you're asking for it."

Harry smiled to himself. He hoped the bosun would get in his way as soon as possible.

9

Maggots Taste Cold

Days passed in a whirl of new experiences. Harry felt as though he worked, ate, and slept in a strange world.

His time was spent working with the gun crews. He worked so long and hard that even in his hammock, his legs felt as though they were still going up and down the deck ladders.

His head spun with new information. He learned about the different kinds of shot that went into the cannons. He learned how the ship relied on the sails and the winds to give it direction and speed.

He rarely saw George, except when they had meals. One of the petty officers had discovered that George could read and write, and since then, George had been put to work by the ship's captain. Harry felt very proud of his friend and was glad that he had been given a gentleman's job.

George was also popular with the seamen; he would read newsletters to them and write letters for them.

At least Harry saw Jack all of the time. He was on the gun crew that Harry monkeyed for. He was the sponger-out of the cannon. They never had time to speak to each other, but it made Harry feel good to know he was there.

What disappointed Harry the most was that he rarely had time to spend on the upper deck. He wanted to look at the sea and feel the salty air on his face. He caught glimpses of the sky through the gunports, but it just wasn't enough.

It was not how he'd imagined it would be.

For one thing, where were the other boys? He didn't go looking for them at mealtimes because he wanted to spend time with George and Jack. While on watch, they were too busy.

Powder monkeys flew around ignoring everything but their precious bag of cartridges. He did this himself. He had met the captain's shoe boy a few times, and the five boys who worked in the galley, but they never really had time to talk.

It was the times he could spend with Billy
that he enjoyed the most. Billy was the young
boy with the wide grin. He worked up on the
top deck, looking after the animals. He and
Harry had become good friends.

Billy was only ten years old. He had stowed
away after his parents had died, and he had
been working on the *Prosperity* for almost
a year.

He had names for each of the pigs, sheep, and chickens that he was looking after. He hated it when the men came and took them away for food.

The last time Harry had climbed up to see Billy, the men in bright-red uniforms had chased him below again.

"Get out of here, you dirty little powder monkey," one called.

Harry had scrambled back down to the lower decks. They had called him "dirty." He looked down at his ragged, dirt-smeared clothes and his bruised and grubby arms. He realized what a pathetic pile of dirt and rags he had become.

He was beginning to feel sorry for himself. "That won't help," he muttered. "I've got to deal with it... I'm just homesick. That's all."

That night he whispered to George as they lay in their hammocks. "When will we go home?" George only snored. Harry didn't believe George was asleep – he just didn't have an answer.

When he rolled out of his hammock a few hours later, Harry felt better. Even if he were homesick, hungry all the time, and worn out from running up and down ladders, one thing was sure. He was going to be the finest powder monkey the *Prosperity* had ever seen.

He stowed away his hammock for the day and munched on a biscuit, ignoring the soft parts, which he knew were maggots. If Jack and everyone else could eat them, then so could he.

When he got home, he would tell his ma something she didn't know: Maggots tasted cold. That would make her laugh. Maybe she'd serve them for supper.

At the end of the next watch, Harry was pleased to see George on the orlop. He was sitting with a group of seamen, reading from a newsletter.

"So what does it mean?" one asked.

"It means that we're going to join Lord Nelson's flagship, *Victory*. We're going to stop the French, once and for all."

"Fighting alongside Lord Nelson," Jack murmured.

"Yes, my friends," George said. "In a few days we will be in a great battle. We're going to war. We're going to save our country."

Harry felt his heart beat faster. He was tired of all the practicing. He was ready for the real thing.

Some of the men cheered, but some who had been in battles before stayed silent. Afterward – long afterward – Harry realized why. They knew that many good men would die, and the unlucky could be some of them.

10

Action Stations

Harry woke with a smile on his face. He had been dreaming of the gunsmith's shop. He was feeding the little monkey, while George wrote in his ledger. Everything was as it should be. He had done a day's work at the chandler's, and he would take his two pennies home to his ma.

The sound of soft voices brought him back to reality. It was George and Jack talking. He listened.

"You've got to promise me, George."

"I really don't know if I can do that," George replied.

"I'm telling you more men have died at the hands of the surgeon than in battle. He takes off your arms or legs simply because he doesn't know what else to do."

Harry heard George give a deep sigh.

"What exactly do you want me to do?" George asked.

"If I get some really bad wounds in the battle, throw me overboard. I'd rather drown in the ocean than get that kind of treatment. Please, George."

Harry tried to peek at the two men without tipping himself from the hammock. He watched them shake hands. Surely George hadn't agreed.

He was suddenly frozen with fear at the thought of losing either of these two good friends. And what about himself? He'd never really thought about death, only the glory of winning and being part of the King's Navy.

Harry noticed that many men were already out of their beds, even though the bell hadn't sounded to start the next watch.

There was a buzz of excited chatter. Men were stowing away their hammocks, stuffing them along the side of the ship as extra protection against gunshots. Porridge had been brought from the galley and put on the tables.

George appeared at the side of Harry's hammock. "Come on, there's a lot to do. We're waiting for a signal from Lord Nelson. We've already sighted the rest of the fleet."

Harry grabbed a biscuit and scrambled up the ladders toward the top deck. Because his watch hadn't really started, he would use the time to go and see Billy.

He dodged the men and the officer on watch and moved toward the animal pen. As usual, Billy was lying in the pen on a pile of straw. The pigs snuffled around him. "Billy, wake up," said Harry.

"Harry, what are you doing here?"

"We've reached the rest of Lord Nelson's fleet. Let's take a look."

Billy scrambled to his feet and followed Harry to the far end of the deck. The two boys climbed up and looked over the side.

The sun was just coming up. About half a mile away, rising and falling on the dark blue water, was a group of the finest fighting ships Harry had ever seen.

The English colors were flying proudly from the mast of the big flagship. It was the HMS *Victory* itself – the ship of Admiral Lord Nelson.

The two boys were speechless. Soon they would be part of the fleet.

The sound of eight bells told them one watch was finished and the next was beginning. Harry told Billy he would try to see him later, then he ran back to the orlop.

The bosun was talking to the men. George stood at his side, holding a sheet of paper in his hand. The men fell silent as George read the message.

"On this, the 21st day of October, in the year of 1805, the Admiral Lord Nelson orders his fleet to prepare for battle. Today there will be battle with the French and Spanish fleets. We will fight to the death. No prisoners will be taken. A drum roll will sound action stations."

Seconds later, men were racing to all parts of the ship. Harry made his way to his gun crew on the middle deck.

He learned from the gun crew that they were off Cape Trafalgar, near the Spanish port of Cadiz. It meant little to him. It was not England, and that was all he understood.

He helped the men spread the decks with wet sand to help prevent the gun crew from slipping.

Then he started his journeys back and forth to the magazine, collecting cartridges and placing them in the salt box. When it was full, the gun captain told him to stand easy. That meant he could take a break until the next order came.

Harry sat with the men, who were eerily quiet. He wondered how Billy would manage, up on the top deck without any protection.

Suddenly he could hear officers arguing. It seemed that Lord Nelson had decided upon a different way of attacking the enemy.

Normally, the English and any enemy fleet would sail alongside each other in parallel lines, firing their rows of cannons at each other.

This time Nelson had said only half the fleet would do this. The other half would come at the enemy from right angles.

One officer, who had been in Nelson's fleet before, said that it sounded crazy. The gun crew began muttering among themselves as they discussed the new plan of action.

"That will mean we can't fire at them until we're really close, and then we'll only have the end of the ship as a target," a sailor said.

"Yes," said Jack, "but the enemy won't be able to shoot at us either. We'll have some kind of chance with our shots. They won't have any."

A few minutes later, a drumroll began. The hairs on Harry's neck stood on end. Then he heard the shout.

"Action stations!"

The battle was about to begin.

11

Fire!

Harry crouched behind the gun crew, shaking with a mixture of fear and excitement. They were waiting for the order to fire.

Through the gunport, he could see one of the line of ships change direction and start sailing at right angles toward the French fleet and their Spanish allies.

A messenger tumbled along the deck with a message for the whole crew – a message from the Admiral Lord Nelson.

"England expects every man to do his duty," cried the messenger.

The words echoed from man to man. Harry heard others take up the cry. "England expects every man to do his duty!" The message found its way through the ship.

Harry felt so proud. England needed him and all the men of the fleet. He would do his very best for England and Lord Nelson.

Suddenly, the air filled with the roar of both English and enemy-ship cannons as they fired on each other.

The gun crew's first shot boomed out, and the great cannon threw itself back in violent recoil.

At the same moment, a splintering sound came from above as chain shot from the enemy wrapped itself around their rigging. Part of the mast came crashing to the deck. Harry saw it hit a crew member. He stood transfixed, wondering what to do.

"Move, powder monkey!" The gun captain yelled at him furiously.

Harry remembered his duties and ran off to the magazine for more cartridges. The leather carrying case, heavy with cartridges, thudded against his hip. He gasped for breath. The roars of the men and the terrifying booms of the guns filled his head and made his teeth ache and his throat shake and vibrate intensely.

Each time he returned to the gun, there were more injured men, but if they could still stand, they stuck to their posts. As he moved from deck to deck, he tried not to look at the men who were crying out in pain, or worse still, lying silent.

The air was thick and heavy with smoke that burned the back of his throat and made him cough. The harder his breathing became, the slower he moved. He took very shallow breaths, trying his best not to inhale too much smoke.

Imitating some of the men, he tore a strip from his shirt and wound it lightly around his mouth.

He filled the salt box for the third time and took a moment to watch the gun crew running out the gun again. Jack passed close to him.

"All right, young lad?" he gasped to Harry. "You're doing great."

Harry grinned. He would run his heart out for men like Jack. He would ignore the noise and the smoke and do his duty.

He took off down the ladders again. This time he moved faster and started repeating Nelson's message to himself, matching the rhythm of his running. "England expects every man to do his duty."

This kept him going, even as he saw the injured men around him.

"England expects…" He was still chanting to himself as he quickly climbed back to the middle deck.

Halfway to his salt box, he stopped in his tracks. Something was very wrong.

There was a gaping hole in the deck where the great black cannon had stood.

Black smoke filled the air. Large sparks floated around his head. He saw some of the gun-crew lying on what was left of the deck. Their injuries were awful. Harry could hardly bear to look at them, but he knew he must see if any of them needed help. Where was Jack? He couldn't bear it if one of those men was Jack.

He crouched down, trembling.

A faint cry for help came to him through the noise of the battle. He looked around him. The cry came again.

It was Jack. He was swinging in midair, hanging from a piece of the broken deck. The beam he was clinging to was bending and creaking dangerously. Far below him were the guns of the lower deck. If he fell, he would be wounded terribly – at best.

"What shall I do?" called Harry, getting as near to the edge as possible.

"Find a rope. Tie it to something strong. Pass the end to me and I'll haul myself up."

Harry looked around frantically.

He found a coil of rope lying just behind his salt box. His hands shook as he pulled out a length. He ran to the side of the ship, tied it to a spar that looked intact, and unrolled the rest of the coil.

"Hurry," Jack called, "I'm about to drop."

As Harry rushed back, there was a loud splintering sound. The wooden spar cracked and began to split.

Harry saw Jack lose the grip with one of his hands and swing wildly.

Quickly, he lowered the rope and Jack reached for it with his free hand. Then the deck gave way completely, throwing Harry onto his back. He screamed as Jack vanished from sight. Harry crept to the gaping hole, hoping wildly that Jack was on the end of the swinging rope.

He was there; white-faced and gasping for breath, but he was safe.

He started to pull himself up. Harry reached forward to help him, but Jack sent him back, fearing they would both go down.

Jack finally scrambled on deck, just as the ship was hit again. There were screams from men at the other end of the deck as pieces of mast and sail crashed down around them. But still, those gun crews who were able continued firing.

Jack and Harry hugged each other. "Thanks, lad. You're a fine shipmate."

Harry's eyes stung with emotion and the heavy smoke.

"Come on," Jack said. "We'd better see if we can help the other guns. Follow me."

They picked their way between the piles of timber and canvas and injured men.

Harry tugged at Jack's arm. "Jack, I want to go and see if Billy's all right."

"No, lad. I've heard the top deck has just about had it. Some of it's gone."

"Well, what about George?" Harry asked.

"Listen," Jack said roughly, "the battle's not over yet. You don't think of others until your duty's done."

"Sorry," Harry murmured.

For the next hour, Harry became powder monkey for gun crew number four. Their own poor boy had been injured. Despite that, this team had been luckier than most, and they still had their gun captain. Jack took over from the rammer who was also injured.

The battle continued. They heard men saying that the ships that had sailed in the new formation had caused great damage to the French and Spanish ships. Some whispered that victory might be in their grasp.

As Harry returned out of breath from another run to the magazine, a rough-looking sailor was waiting for him.

"You the powder monkey who's got a friend called George? The one who reads and writes?"

Harry nodded.

"Well, he wants to see you up on the next deck. He's been hit. He's been hit bad."

12

Victory at a Price

As soon as Harry found someone to replace him, he raced up to the next deck. He dodged between the dying and the injured until he found George. He was propped up in a sitting position, with one wounded arm hanging helplessly at his side. His face was badly cut.

"George, I'm here. What happened? Are you all right?"

"Never mind that," George said. He called to an officer. "This is the lad I told you about. He can write the messages down for me."

An officer shoved paper, pen, and ink at Harry, and looked out of the *porthole* toward the flagship. "Just write down the signals as I call them out to you. Do you understand?" the officer said.

Harry nodded nervously. He watched his friend's face grow gray with pain.

Minutes passed. There seemed to be less firing from both the *Prosperity* itself and the enemy.

Now and then, men would cheer and cry out as they watched French and Spanish ships take hits or begin to sink.

Suddenly, the officer began to read a signal to Harry. "A – great – victory – is – in – sight. Our – gallant – Admiral – Lord – Nelson – lies – dying – from – a – sniper's – bullet."

Harry and George looked at each other. A wonderful leader was dying. The Battle of Trafalgar was almost won, but the hero of the hour wouldn't live through it.

"Take it to the captain, Harry," George said weakly.

A minute later, he and another lad were sent off running around the ship, giving the news. There were no cheers about the victory, only sadness at the news about Lord Nelson.

Harry made his way to the top of the ship – he had to find Billy.

A sorry sight met his eyes. The deck was almost destroyed, and only parts of the little pen remained. There was no sign of Billy.

Harry bit his lip hard. He knew that Billy would have stayed with his animals, but surely he couldn't be dead.

Harry called out as loudly as he could. "Billy! Billy! Where are you?"

Harry went over to where the pigs lay and stood in silence as men moved around him.

Something stirred beneath the heavy weight of the pigs. Suddenly, a hand appeared and reached out.

With a cry of joy, Harry grasped the hand and pulled. Within seconds, a small boy wriggled free.

"Billy!" Harry cried. "You're alive!"

Billy smiled. "There was a blast and I got knocked off my feet. Then the pigs fell on me. The poor things saved me, really."

Back on the middle deck, the bosun was giving orders. Soon the men would be able to stand down and get some food and rest.

It was good to be alive.

Several weeks later, Harry and Billy sat on deck, counting the maggots in their biscuits. George was sitting near them with his arm in a sling and much better color in his face.

Jack, who had come through with only a few scratches, slept in his hammock.

They had been to Gibraltar for repairs, but once again they were at sea.

The ship rolled gently. The wind whistled around the rigging. They were going home.

13

There's No Place Like Home

People lined the quay as the *Prosperity* sailed into harbor. News of their victory and the death of Lord Nelson had reached England on the fifth day of November.

Harry strained his eyes to see if his ma was there. George stood by himself, looking for his family. Surely, after their disappearance, they would have guessed where the two young men had gone. Such things had happened often enough before.

Even though Billy had no family of his own to look for, he too stretched over the rail, scanning the quay.

"It's Ma!" cried Harry. "I'm sure I can see Ma."

"There's Shadrach, and Mr. Mumford," called George.

Minutes later, Harry tumbled into his mother's arms, not even attempting to hide his tears of joy. They hugged each other over and over again.

"Oh, I've hoped beyond hope you were on this ship today. I was so afraid you were gone forever," she cried.

Harry dragged Billy forward to meet his ma.

She was charmed immediately by his friendly grin. "You'll stay with us," she said.

Shadrach and Mr. Mumford came over and shook Harry by the hand. Shadrach slapped him on the shoulder. "Well, I suppose earning two pennies a day will be too tame for you now, eh?" he said.

"No, sir. I'll start again tomorrow if I can bring Billy too," Harry said. The men laughed.

"You mean you're not signing up for another sea trip?" Mr. Mumford said.

Harry blushed, but said nothing.

"Well, before you go off home," the gunsmith went on, "I've got something for you back at the shop."

In the back room, Mr. Mumford took the sampler down from the wall. He pointed to the beautifully embroidered words.

"There's no place like home," he said. "Let this remind you."

He handed it to Harry. Harry thanked him, but he knew he didn't really need it. He had his own reminders; too many of them. His dreams would be filled with them.

They'd be very different from the dreams he'd had before going to sea and to war. He never wanted to handle a gun again, unless it was to clean it.

"And another thing," Mr. Mumford said. "Do you remember what I said you could do the next time we met?"

Harry looked puzzled. Then it came to him. "The little monkey!" he cried. "You said I could name the monkey."

"That's right, lad."

Mr. Mumford went into the other room and returned with the small creature. She chattered to herself as he handed her over to Harry.

Harry laughed as she began picking through his hair with her tiny fingers.

"Well, lad. She's all yours if you want her. So what's it to be? Give her a name."

"I've got the perfect name for her," Harry
said, smiling at everyone.

The little monkey looked at Harry with her
bright, beady eyes.

"I'll call her Powder," he said.

Glossary

bosun – the boatswain, or an officer on a ship in charge of looking after its equipment

chandler – a dealer who sells specific kinds of supplies to the public

handspike – a bar used as a lever to move heavy objects

orlop deck – the lowest deck in a ship that has more than four decks

porthole – an opening in the side of a ship

powder monkey – a boy on a fighting ship who brings gunpowder to the cannons

quay – a landing place where ships can load and unload

wad – a soft plug used to hold gunpowder in a cannon

About the Author

I'm a primary school teacher, so most of my writing has to be done during school vacations. The story of Harry the powder monkey first came to me while I was visiting a museum. There was a life-size reconstruction of an old fighting ship. I stood looking at it for a long time.

In my mind I could see the many young boys who were used on board those ships to do hard and dangerous jobs. Over the next few days, Harry's story came to me. Then, after a lot of research, I wrote *The Powder Monkey*.

Maureen Rylance